Technical analysis of stock market

Copyright © 2020 by SHAIKH JAVED. All Rights Reserved.
Published Digitally by Eagle Corp India. India.

No part of this publication may be reproduced, stored in a retrieval system, or transmitted in any form or by any means, electronic, mechanical, photocopying, recording, scanning, without either the prior written permission of the Publisher, or authorization through payment of the appropriate per-copy fee to the Eagle Corp India, Nanded Maharashtra-431605, Email: eaglecorpind@gmail.com. Requests to the Publisher for permission should be addressed By Email.

The information contained in this guide is for informational purposes only. Any legal or financial advice I give is my opinion based on my own experience. You should always seek the advice of a professional before acting on something I have published or recommended. there are some links contained in this guide that I may benefit from financially.

By reading this guide, you agree that myself and my company is not responsible for the success or failure of your business decisions relating to any information presented in this guide.

Please make sure that while making any business decisions based on this guide, you should verify each and everything and you are responsible for your own actions.

SR NO.	CONTENTS
1.	BASIC FOR BEGINNERS
	WHAT IS SHARE MARKET?
	SEGMENTS
	ORDER PLACEMENT
	MOVEMENTS OF MARKET
	BREAKOUTS
	MONEY MANAGEMENT AND MARGIN
2.	WHAT IS SUPPORT AND RESISTANCE
	SUPPORT
	RESISTANCE
	USING S&R TO PREDICT MARKET
3.	THE CANDLE STICK PATTERN
	WHAT IS CANDLE STICK PATTERN
	ENGULFING
	HAMMERS
	DOJI
4.	ANALYSIS
	RSI
	MACD
	ADX
	MOVING AVERAGE
	BOLLINGER BANDS
	TIME FRAMES
5.	SOME FUNDAMENTALS
	SCOPE OF COMPANY
	EARNING REPORTS
6.	TRADE AND TIPS
	ENTRY
	EXIT
	TIPS
	CONTACT & SUPPORT

1. Basic for beginners

What is share market?
"It is a place where shares of public listed companies are traded" Or "A place where investors can buy and sell shares."

What is a share?
A certificate that represents partial ownership in a company.

Segments:

Equity
shares offered by companies in return for money, are called equities. One unit of equity is equal to one share which means you can buy or sell a single share of equity of a company in listed price.

Commodity
A commodity is buying and selling of raw or primary products. Ex(gold, crude oil, silver, etc). A unit of commodity comes with a lot size of respected product.
Ex: if you buy crude oil you have to buy a lot size of 100 under the listed price.

Feature and options (F&O)

A feature is a right to buy or sell any underlying security at a future date at a pre determined price.

And an options contract gives buyer the right, but he is under no obligation to buy or sell the asset. Whereas the seller of the options contract is under obligation to buy or sell the asset based on the option contract buyer's decision.

To buy any f&o you have to choose it according to the strike price of that respected index.

ex: if you want to trade on nifty index and price of the nifty is ₹12000 then at the money strike price is nifty12000 so you can trade according to the option price low or high respect to time of the contract expiration.

Order placement:
Following are the aspects while placing an order

Type of product or validity of shares:
Margin Intraday square off (MIS) or Intraday:
Intraday is nothing but validity of shares to day only, this means you only have rights to buy and sell a share during single market day which will automatically end at market end (Indian market time is 9:15am to 3:30pm for Equity and F&O and for commodity is 10am to 11:30pm)

In this type you can place a buy order of a share at a price say ₹100 and then sell it when it go up say ₹108, so you make ₹8 per share.

The benefit of this type is you can place a sell order of a share without buying it first. And when price go down you can buy it. Ex: you can place a sell order of share having a price of ₹145 and when the price go down to ₹135 you can buy it, by this way you make ₹10 per share.

Delivery or cash and carry (cnc):
In this type you will have rights to sell your shares when you want which means you are not restricted to single market day but you have to buy it first.

Order types

Market (mkt):
In this type when you place an buy or sell order it will be executed at market price of the respective product.
Ex: if your buy order for x stock at market price and the current price of the x share is ₹200 your order will execute at ₹200.

LIMIT (LMT):
this type is most common because in this type when you place an order you have to enter the price value at what price you want the share.
Ex: if your sell order for X with LIMIT order at ₹213 and X's current price is ₹211, so when the price comes to ₹213 your order will be executed.

stop loss LIMIT (SL LMT):
stop loss is nothing but an auto generated order on your instructions if share price move against your target.
In this type when you place an buy or sell order with LIMIT you can place stop loss by which when your share go in wrong direction it will generate the sell or buy order respectively.

Ex: if your buy order for X with LIMIT is ₹1033 and you place stop loss of ₹1020, so if your share go down to ₹1020 then a sell order for X will be generated and will be executed automatically.

Similarly, if your sell order for X with LIMIT is ₹1040 and you place stop loss of ₹1050, so if your share go up to ₹1050 then a buy order for X will be generated and will be executed automatically.

stop loss MARKET (SL MKT):

In this type when you place an buy or sell order with MARKET price you can place stop loss by which when your share go in wrong direction it will generate the sell or buy order respectively.

Order complexity or variety:

Regular or simple order:

In This type you only place order of CNC or intraday with no extra instructions.

Cover order (co):

In this type stop loss is compulsory and only available in MIS orders.

Bracket order (oco):

In this type a buy or sell order of LIMIT with stop loss and target plus an trailing stop loss all placed simultaneously. Only for MIS orders.

Trailing stop loss is nothing but the increasing in stop loss price value by your entered value with respect to increase in share price.

Ex: if you buy X stock with LIMIT order of ₹105 and place stop loss of ₹98, target of ₹108 and trailing stop loss of 1, so when your share goes high to ₹107 your stop loss value increases to ₹100.

After market order (AMO):

after market order are the orders placed after the market closed i.e. after 3:30 pm and till pre-market open i.e. 9am.(indian time)

This are available for both cnc and MIS, only use this if you forecasted correctly.

VALIDITY orders:

Day:
In This type order will be executed anytime till market close.

IOC:
Order will be executed at current time with specified price if not order will be cancelled automatically.

Movements of market:

the movement of market depend upon supply and demand and volume traded

BULLISH:

above chart shows movement of market to upside this is callled bullish movement.

The green candles shows that price is rising up and red candle shows down of the price.

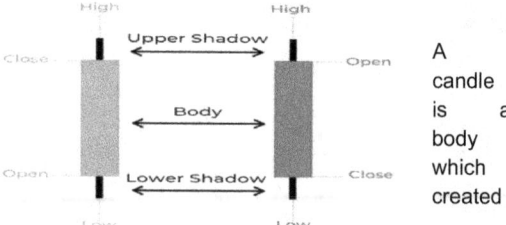

A candle is a body which created

during observation time due to trade, green candle opens low and closes high and red candle opens high and closes low, above chart shows 10 minutes of observation time which means each candle is made in 10 minutes of trade.

BEARISH:

above chart shows movement of market to downside this is called bearish movement.

We will study types of candles in detail later.

Breakouts:
a breakout is market condition when the movement of a stock beyond an identified level of resistance or support, which is usually followed by heavy volumes and an increased amount of volatility.

A true breakout always shows heavy volume change, if a breakout appears with high volatility but low volume change then it is a false breakout or a trap at that time avoid trade.

Money management and Margin:

Money management is nothing but how you invest your earnings, a smart trader should always have multiple source of income so that if you losses your investment you can recover it.

Never invest your 100% available money, invest half or 1/3 rd of available money so that you can always minimize your loss by making average of your invested value or by making another trade.

Margin:

for trading in share market you have to open Demat account with a broker, most of the broker gives you margin of a particular multiplayer on your total investment value for MIS (some of them gives for cnc too).

Ex: if you have ₹5000 and if your broker is giving you x15 margin then

5000x15 = ₹75,000 it means you can buy or sell shares in MIS for about ₹75,000 with just the investment of ₹5000.

2. What is support and resistance
support:

support is the area on the chart which shows that the buyers are pushing the price higher, the white line on the chart shows support but support is not a line its an area where bulls try to push price higher. If the price continues to return to support area it will break and price will fall, so you have to self Analyse the support on different charts

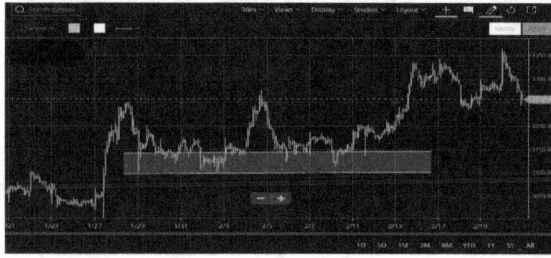

Above chart show how you can make an support on the chart, try to identify different support as in live trading the support changes every time so you have to identify where the bulls are trying to stop price fall.

Resistance:

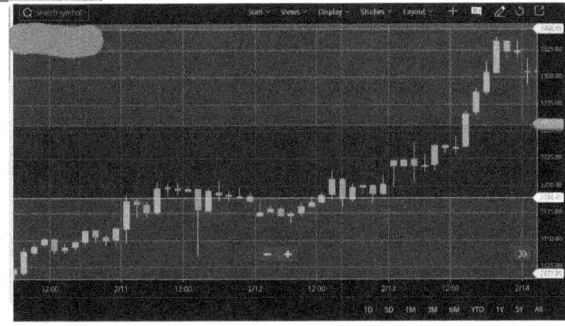

Resistance is an area on the chart which shows that the sellers are pushing the price lower, the white and red line on the chart shows resistance but again resistance is not a line its an area where bears try to push price lower. If the price continues to return to resistance area it will break and price will rise.

The following chart shows how to draw resistance on the chart, so prepare yourself so that in the live market you can make it quick.

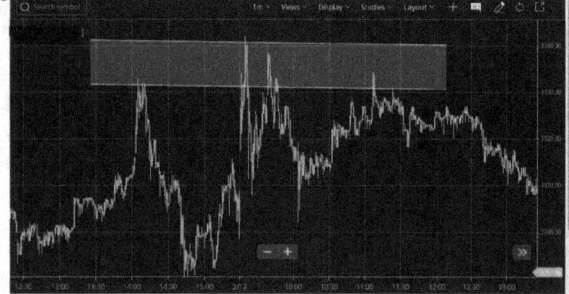

Using S&R to predict market:

the main reason of studying support & resistance is to forecast the trend of the stock, market always moves from support to resistance or resistance to support.

If the support gets tested again and again then it will break the support and if the resistance is tested again and again it will break the resistance.

When support gets break look for selling opportunity and when resistance gets break look for buying opportunity, similarly when price returns from resistance sell and when it returns from support buy.

3. The candle stick pattern
what is candle stick pattern:

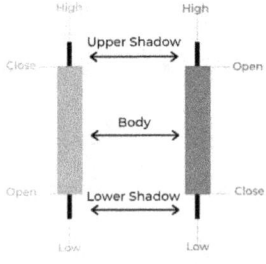

a candle stick is formed when trading of shares happen in a particular time, it consist of four points

Open: the opening price
High: the highest price over a period of time
Low: the lowest price over a period of time
Close: the closing price

Now you will learn some of candle stick patterns which reverses the trend

Engulfing
Bullish:

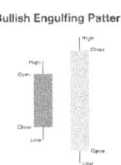

A Bullish Engulfing Pattern is a two candle pattern, the first candle is bearish and the other is bullish. This means buyers took control and now the price is going up.

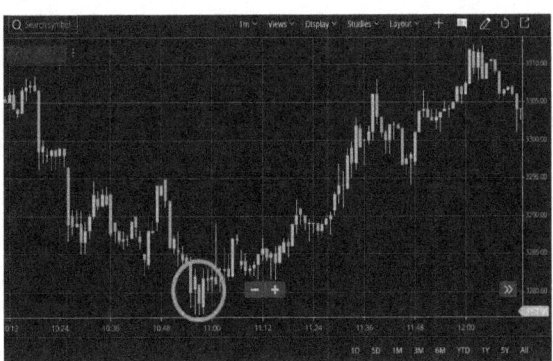

Bearish:

A Bearish Engulfing Pattern is a two candle pattern, the first candle is bullish and the other is bearish. This means sellers took control and now the price is going down.

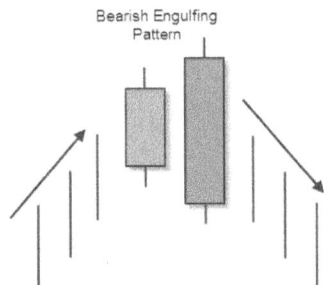

Hammers
Bullish Hammer:

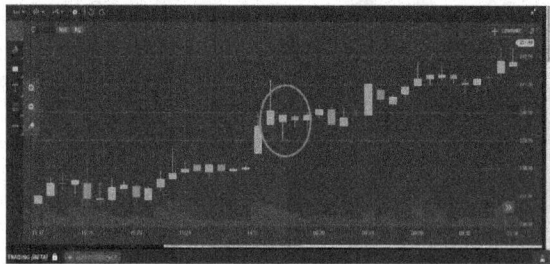

A hammer is a single bullish candle which shows that buyers are in control and price refuse to go down, which means it will go up, it can only be seen in lower time frame(Ex: 1 minute) But if hammer appears it does not fully define a reverse trend so you have to put more thing to confirm your entry.

Bearish Hammer:

A Bearish hammer or shooting star is a single candle which shows that sellers are in control and price refuse to go up, Which means it will go down.
don't make your entry without confirming the trend.

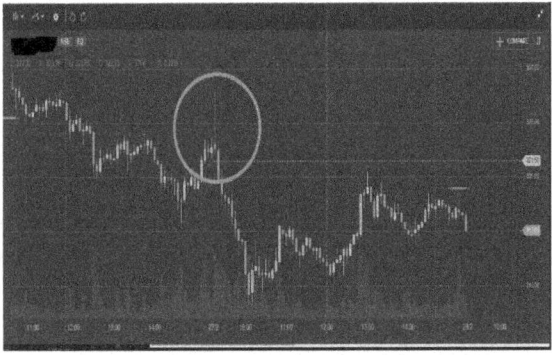

DOJI

a doji is the type of candle stick pattern which shows that neither buyer nor seller are in control.

Gravestone Doji:

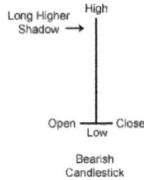

A gravestone doji is a bearish candle stick pattern which means sellers are in control and now price is going to fall.

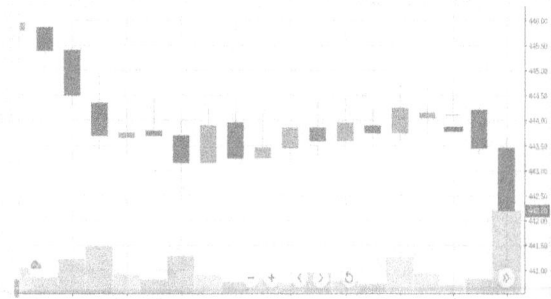

Dragonfly doji:

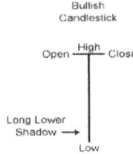

A Dragonfly doji is a bullish candle stick pattern which means

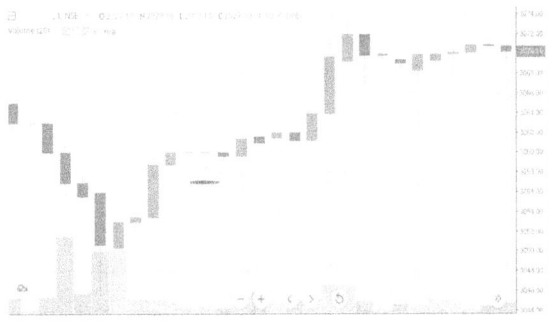

buyers are in control and now price is going up.
Now you have learned some of the candle stick patterns, use these patterns as your entry in trade but before check where the price is going using support and resistance, if price is

going from support to resistance and one of the bullish candle stick pattern appears and if price is going from resistance to support and one of the bearish candle stick pattern appears then only make entry in the trade.

4. Analysis

following are some studies of forecasting the trade, you can add this on your brokers provided app or website. using following studies you can make your own strategies.

Rsi:

rsi is a type of study of chart

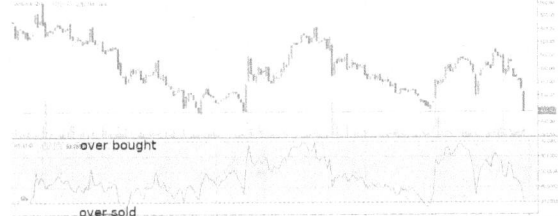

This is a very powerful tool you can actually rely on, this shows the over sold and over bought of the stock, by this you can make strategies.

MACD:
Another powerful tool is Macd. The red bars are movement.

The movement of market can be observed by Macd, if the movement is positive then market is going upward for sure, and if the movement is negative the market is going downward.

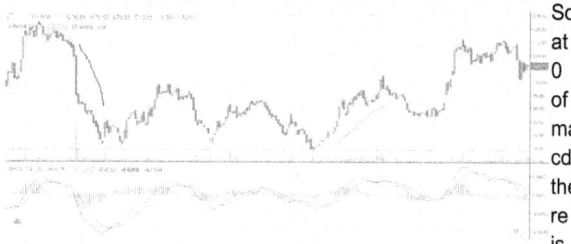

So at 0 of macd there is

mean if the movement crosses mean in downward look for sell and if the macd crosses mean in upward look for buy.

ADX:
a tool to analysis how volatile the trend is.

Using adx you

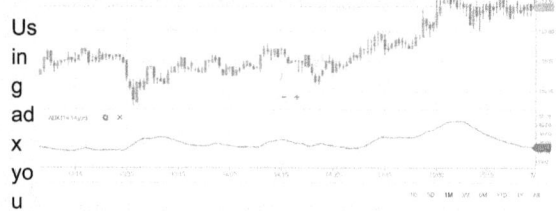

can observe that the volatility of the trend is high or low, you can look for trading opportunity like if the adx is high then use bollinger bands to enter.

Moving averages (m.a):

moving average is a average of price over a period of time, this is shown by line on the chart.

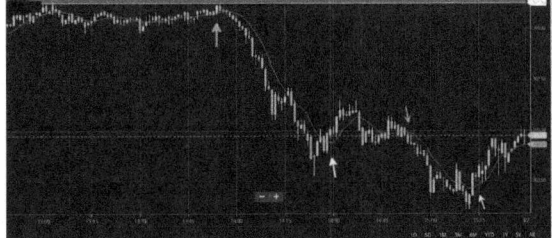

Above chart shows 200 day moving average, moving average (m.a) act as support or resistance on that basis we can make some strategies as follows:above chart uses a 9 m.a, you can observe the 9 m.a is acting as a support and resistance for the price and by using that you can make your entry.

- Use 200 m.a and 50 m.a if you are trading in cnc
- Use 24m.a, 9 m.a if you are trading in intraday

Bollinger Bands:

Bollinger bands shows three simple m.a of 20 day period, the middle band is a simple m.a and other two bands upper and lower are 20 day m.a with +/- deviation.

As the price touches the upper m.a it means over bought of stock and if the price touches the lower m.a it means over sold of stock.

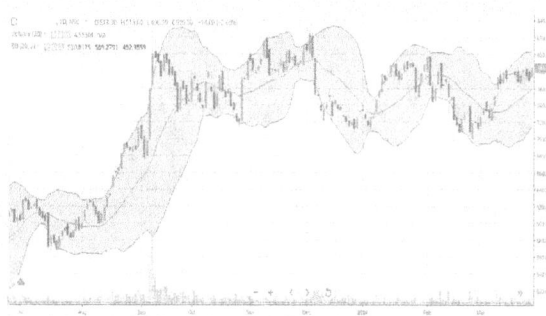

TIME FRAMES:

The time frame is an important factor while analyzing the market and the chart, time frame depend upon which type of trading you want.

- If you are considering for intraday then use short period analysis and use weekly and daily chart for it.
- If you are considering cnc then use long period analysis like yearly and monthly chart.

5. SOME FUNDAMENTALS:

Fundamental Analysis is not for cnc or long term only but it is useful for short term or intraday also.

SCOPE OF COMPANY

Scope of any company is very important factor is we are thinking of investing for long term or for swing trading, if you see there construction is happening in large scale so you can think of the companies which provide raw construction material, or you want to analyze an X company which make part of an automobile and that company collaborated with a foreign company or is selling their product to a popular brand you can think of this companies to rise their values in share market.
You have to analyze what kind of scope a company have and how you are gonna make profit from it.

EARNING REPORTS

you can have a rough idea about what is the financial health of the company by the earning reports of the company.

These reports include net income, earning per share, net sale, and earning from operations.

Analyze these quarterly report (4-month) and you can forecast how financially strong the company will be.

The term earning per share (eps) is the most important term in earning reports.

Eps can give you idea about what should be the share price of the company and what will be the share price.

Just do the math:

'(average of 5 year value of eps of a company) X 25'

(ex; (0.5+2.5+3+1.6+2)/5=1.92 then 1.92 x 25 = 48)

If you get a value(say Z) below current market price of that company then you can buy those share for long term until it reaches Z, and if you get a value higher than the current market price of that company then it is over valued so there may be chances of price fall.

The concept of above formulae is that a company can give you 25% profit.

6. TRADE AND TIPS:

After analyzing and understanding all of the above methods don't jump directly to Battlefield, first train your self for the war.

What this means is first paper trade, use a pen and a paper then check charts and analyze stocks then just write down the price you want to buy or sell then write down the stop loss and target and if your stock performs well and your analysis works or not then, if your analysis works and stocks perform well as you expected then only trade on real market with minimum value say ₹2000/- or ₹5000/- any amount that you can easily manage to recover yourself

if you loss money, but if you see yourself losing in paper trading then I suggest you try hard to make profit in paper trade. You can only win if you make your own strategies and choose the segment you can understand so work on that.

To see chart of stocks use your brokers app, website.
Or if you don; have an account then open it on upstox, zerodha(for indians), or use market plus or investing.com.

Entry:
First analyze then make paper trade then go to the real war, place your order in your brokers app, website with proper selection of segment, type of order, complexity, stop loss and target.

Remember its not a video game which you can complete a level and go forward or any of those binary trading app so that you can trade by walking on the street, this is real money we are talking about leave all your work aside, try calm yourself, sit comfortably and then only place your because there no turning back from that after you place order.

I have seen people losses their money only because they think they can make money while doing their other work, now I am not telling you to sit for 1-2 hours, just make yourself available for a small time if you are doing intraday and for CNC prepare yourself before market opens.

Now what you have placed an order make sure that your target must be 0.5-1% of the stock price and stoploss of 1-2% of the stock price for intraday.

Ex: x is at 100 you place order so put your target of sell at 101 and sl of 99, or target of buy at 99 and sl of 101.

but the hardest part is now where you have to wait for your target to achieve, you can only win if you have done it successfully in your paper trade, the only thing here is you have actual money on the bit. You have to train your mind so that you could hold up to your target and that is reason we are putting small targets and bearable stoploss. You can increase your target and sl by continuously practicing and making new strategies.

Exit:

Your order is processed successfully and you got the target its time to exit, if you haven't placed your order as an bracket order then I suggest you place exit order of mkt type or at market price to instantly exit from your positions list in brokers app or website.

Exiting is as important as entering because if the market is volatile you won't get a chance to exit at your price so try to avoid trading that day as its safe to not lose money because you can't exit at your expected price.

As a wise man once said " market is like river you just have to put a glass and take out with whatever you got", because instant high speed flow can drown you, so don't forget to get out of that before the big bulls and bears watch you.

If you see that the trend is changing and buyers or sellers are going against you then don't wait for the target to achieve just exit, but first you have to be 100% sure that the trend is reversed so use trend following analysis to check whether you are in right position, because if you just exit without any profit or much less its not a profit at all which means that loss.

This doesn't mean that you see one or two red or green candles and just exit no you should analyze well that you are in the direction of trend or not.

Always exit before 3 PM (IST 5:30) or 15 minutes before market close if you are doing MIS so that your brokers shouldn't have to

square off you because they will they extra money for square off. So
exit from your position early.

Tips:

- At first trade between 9:15 to 9:45 it's the best time beginners can learn(the first half hour of market opening)
- After you master the strategies you can play by those strategies but don't make your own rules because market always run by its own rules.
- Always try to analyze before market opening try to forecast some stocks before they open it will make you understand what is working and what is not.
- At don't try to put AMO orders its risky.
- Try to order in bracket order type it will give you more options.
- Try to make paper trade you first lesson it will give a rough idea of how you can play an investor role in real market.
- All of the above analysis and methods are irrespective of external conditions which means these analysis can change if any external condition happens with large number of investors at the same time.
- External conditions can be environmental conditions, natural disaster, elections, global pandemic, recession.
- These conditions do affect the market and I suggest you trade carefully.
- Any external condition can affect an investor directly like a natural disaster can make some healthy investors to exit their trade which leads to fall of a company.

- Or an election can make investor back support economically which may lead to jump up any company with huge volume.
- Guess we never know which thing can happen but we can have a rough idea about the rise and fall of market.
- Never I repeat never think share market is like touching some buttons and making money, no its about discipline and sincerity towards making money.
- You have to follow the path which was followed by big bulls and bears of the market to be successful.
- Don't forget "one man's loss is another man's gain", be that another man.
- Trust yourself and trust your strategy even if you have to wait till market end, unless the trend is reversed.

- Most of the trader forget two rules of the market first is never borrow or loan money and invest and second is never invest someone else's money whether that person is your best friend or a co-worker.
- A smart trader always have another source of income so whenever he fall he can support himself.
- Don't invest all of your money only invest 1/3 so if you fall you can make average and exit with minimum loss.
- Start with taking small profits say 5-10% of your total investment and when you gain experience then gradually increase the profit.

Contact & support:

That's it follow the guide carefully on your own risk this guide is only for learning purpose, though it will jump start your career as an entrepreneur, for further guidance and any assistance email us at eaglecorpind@gmail.com .

TO HELP PEOPLE UNDERSTAND STOCK MARKET WE HAVE DESIGNED SOME COURSES WHICH CAN GIVE YOU DETAIL KNOWLEDGE ABOUT HOW STOCK MARKET WORKS AND HOW YOU CAN MAKE MONEY
WE HAVE DESIGNED THREE DIFFERENT COURSES,
1) TECHNICAL ANALYSIS
2) FUNDAMENTAL ANALYSIS
3) MASTER COURSE(INCLUDE ABOVE TWO + F&O + LONG TERM STRATEGIES + MUTUAL FUNDS)
FOR COURSES YOU CAN CONTACT US ON EMAIL OR ON INSTAGRAM @eaglecorpind.

To recommend this book share the links from where you purchased this book like (amazon kindle or google play or payhip.com) links or those who can't afford to pay ☐251/- or equivalent an app "Technical Analysis of stock market" by Eaglecorp will be available soon on platforms(android, ios, windows and linux) for free, so please share this book with your friends and relatives thank you and Have a Profitable Future Ahead.